I0381101

Linda Sue Svoboda

A Gift For Alia

By

Linda Sue Svoboda

PUBLISHED by PARABLES
Earthly Stories with a Heavenly Meaning

Linda Sue Svoboda

A Gift For Alia
Linda Sue Svoboda

Published By Parables
June, 2020

All Rights Reserved. No part of this book may be reproduced or utilized in any form or by any means, electronic or mechanical, including photocopying, recording, or by any information storage and retrieval system, without permission in writing from the author. Unless otherwise noted all Bible translations are drawn from the NASB translation of the Bible.

ISBN 978-1-951497-68-2
Printed in the United States of America

Readers should be aware that Internet Web sites offered as citations and/or sources for further information may have been changed or disappeared between the time this was written and the time it is read.

A Gift For Alia

By

Linda Sue Svoboda

PUBLISHED by PARABLES

Earthly Stories with a Heavenly Meaning

Linda Sue Svoboda

A Gift For Alia

Dedication

This book is lovingly dedicated to my wonderful family, who has always shown me God's precious and unfailing love. They have also encouraged me to pursue my dreams. I am incredibly grateful for them.

Linda Sue Svoboda

Table of Contents

Chapter 1 -   p.3

Chapter 2 -   p.7

Chapter 3 -   p.11

Chapter 4 -   p.15

Chapter 5 -   p.19

Chapter 6 -   p.21

Chapter 7 -   p.25

Chapter 8 -   p.29

Chapter 9 -   p.33

Chapter 10 -   p.37

Chapter 11 -   p.45

Chapter 12 -   p.47

Chapter 13 -   p.53

Chapter 14 -   p.55

Chapter 15 -   p.59

Chapter 16 -   p.63

Chapter 17 -   p.65

Chapter 18 -   p.67

Chapter 1

She was in the bars every weekend. She didn't know why she was there, or why it appealed to her so much. The smell of the smoke was comforting, and the loud hip-hop music was soothing in a strange way. This was so unlike the environment in which she had been raised. Her parents had taken her to church every Sunday, a place that should be inviting and welcoming. Unfortunately, it turned out that it was just the opposite for her. While she was pondering this, she heard her friend, Jacie, say," Hey, Alia, come over here. There's someone I want you to meet."

She turned around and saw a very handsome man staring at her. She smiled at him, as he led her onto the dance floor. He had a perfect smile, and very easily said to her," Where have you been all my life, gorgeous?" Alia was mesmerized by the charm in his voice, and by the tailored clothes he wore. As they danced throughout the evening, Alia took in every word that he said, and felt like she was in a daze. They hung out throughout the evening, but after they said good bye, Alia felt an ache in her heart. She wondered if she would ever see him again, and for some strange reason, it was ok with her if she didn't. She knew in her heart that she wanted more than just a glamorous evening of dancing. Although that was fun, she was tired of superficial guys who only wanted to flatter her. After dancing awhile with him, she became more confused than ever.

"Why in the world do I keep coming here?" Alia asked herself. She realized that she felt extremely empty, and she wasn't listening to the nonstop chitter chatter that Jacie was saying. She suddenly knew in her heart that she wanted something more, but she was scared. She had had so many boyfriends over the last couple of years, and she was hurt. She thought especially of Steve. She had met him at a bar, but he was 10 years older than she was. He knew all the "right" things to say, and all the wonderful places to take her. She fell quickly in love with him, but after a while he wanted to move on, and it broke her heart.

"Alia, are you listening to me?" Jacie asked impatiently.

"I'm sorry Jacie. My mind is wandering a little. Would you mind if we just went home? I am not feeling the best, and I need to lay down for a while."

"Sure Alia, we can do that. Is there anything that I can help you with?" Jacie asked with concern.

Alia noticed that Jacie had such a concerned look on her face, but Alia just shook her head and said, "No, I will be ok. I just have a lot of thinking to do."

After Jacie dropped her off at her apartment, Alia went right to sleep. She slept like a rock, and didn't wake up until the middle of the morning. "Maybe I can make it to the late church service," she thought to herself. She got ready quickly, and raced off to the church that she had attended since she was a little girl.

Everyone was just starting to enter the small church. With its absence of stained glass windows, Alia thought the building looked darker than usual. She then wondered if her heart was darker as well.

As she looked for her parents, she noticed people staring at her. They were not friendly glances though. People were whispering, looking unapprovingly, and turning away.

"What are they saying?" Alia asked herself. Then she realized what they may have been saying. Word gets around, and she knew that she had not been too faithful when it came to her churchgoing.

The Pastor's sermon was long, but Alia only caught one thing. He talked about being faithful to God. Throughout his sermon, he kept looking at her. It was not a friendly look, but rather it was a frown. She realized that she had been in the wrong places, that she had the wrong friends, and that she had been living a wrong life. She felt extremely guilty, and she did not know how to fix it. After the sermon, she felt awful. She looked around to find her Mom and Dad. She spotted them towards the front. She felt like running far away from the building, but instead she ran into her Mother's arms.

"So good to see you honey!" her Mom said with a big smile.

"So glad that you could make it," her Dad said while giving her a huge hug. Alia gave them both a big hug, and was very thankful that they were her parents.

Her parents asked her if they could take her out to eat, and she said that would be wonderful. Over lunch they had a great visit, and Alia felt that she could share freely with them about what was going on in her life. She told them that she loved the kids that she took care of during the day as a nanny. She talked about the funny things they said and did. She told them that she was going out on the weekends with Jacie. She didn't tell them everything about the guys that she was seeing though. She felt bad keeping that to herself, but she didn't know if they would understand that part. Part of her wanted to, but she didn't feel ready to talk about that part of her life to her parents yet. She said a little prayer to God, that sometime she could share that part of her life with them. A glimmer of hope suddenly came to her, and she knew that they might possibly understand.

9

Linda Sue Svoboda

Chapter 2

Blake Ellison was such a hard-working man. He got to his job at the plant before 5 a.m., and he made sure that all the windows he made were absolutely perfect. He was a decent man with a lot of friends. But he kept to himself mostly. He brought his headphones, and listened to his music.

"What are you listening to today Blake?" his friend Martin asked.

"Hi Martin. I am listening to one of Pastor Dave's sermons. He's talking about forgiveness." Blake said with a ready smile.

"Ok, I should have known," Martin said with a grin. "That's good for you, but I'm not into that stuff. I like to live for the day, and not worry about sermons. But if it makes you happy, then good for you." With a pat on Blake's back, Martin moved on. Blake found himself praying for Martin, that he would want to learn more about God, and want to talk about having a relationship with him.

He felt such a peace that even though a lot of his co-workers were swearing, and telling inappropriate stories, he didn't have to be a part of that. He was hoping and praying that he could make a difference at the plant. He knew there would come a time when he would have to explain why he was so different from the rest of the crew. So he just prayed that he would be ready. It was hard for him to tell his story. He just hoped that his actions would shine a light towards the One who had made him different. Because sometimes he didn't have all the right words to say, but he knew Someone who would help him say the right things. It was his Best Friend, and he was so thankful to know Him.

After Blake got off work, he was exhausted, but he knew he had something very special to do. It was his turn to volunteer at the nursing home. It was a place where he learned so much from the residents. They had so much to share, but his favorite was his own grandmother, Dolly.

Blake got to the cafeteria, and spotted the short, white-haired lady. As he got closer to her, her arms went up and she said, "There's my sweet boy," with a big smile on her face. Blake bent over and gave her a great, big hug.

"Hi Grandma," he said joyfully. "It's good to see you."

"It's always so good to see you too. You are such a precious boy." With that hearty welcome, they started talking. He remembered their talks from previous days, because they sparked his curiosity. She always had stories to tell about his ancestors, and he loved to hear about them.

"Today, I am going to tell you about your great Uncle Pete. He had so many friends, and was well liked by everyone. He always had a joke to share, and he made everyone laugh. He did have a downfall, and that was he liked his liquor. He drank so much when he was by himself, and it was so sad to see. Being his sister, I tried everything to help him. He drank so much, but no one knew why. But Blake, I think I may have figured it out." Grandma said with a sad smile.

Blake sat up taller in his chair, wondering what his sweet Grandma was going to say.

"Even though Pete had a lot of friends, I still feel there was a hole in his heart for something deeper. He had a longing for a real relationship. And to my knowledge, he never had that." Dolly shook her head sadly and her eyes welled up with tears.

"I told him about Jesus, and how he can take away any pain or heart-ache. He didn't want to listen to that. I just kept praying for him. I just hope that somehow he turned to Jesus before he died." Dolly said.

"I really hope he did Grandma." Blake said with emotion.

"I do have to tell you about his funeral though. It was at a medium sized church, but we all had no idea how many people would come. It filled up so fast, and there was a line all the way around the block. People just wanted to come in. He touched so many lives. People were telling us stories of what Pete said or did for them. They shared how he had helped them. It was so encouraging to us, but I kept thinking that I just wished that Pete could hear all of this." Grandma Dolly said.

"You know, Grandma, it really makes me want to show those around me how much I appreciate them. It makes me want to tell those around me how much I care about them and how much they have touched my life," Blake said with determination. "And I am starting with you, Grandma. You have taught me so much about life, and how to live for God. You have been there for me, and for that I am so very thankful. Thanks so much, Grandma."

Dolly looked at Blake with tears in her eyes. "I love you, my precious boy. Thanks for being such an amazing grandson."

After a tearful hug, Blake went to the front desk to see how he could help serve in the nursing home today. He just prayed that he could make a difference in somebody's life today. He didn't realize it, but he already did.

10

Linda Sue Svoboda

Chapter 3

"Hey Alia, come over here!" A little girl with blonde pigtails shouted. Alia turned around and saw sweet little Kenzie holding out her arms to her. "I found a beautiful butterfly! Do you want to hold him? We could also name him something!"

Alia took the butterfly and said, "Kenzie, you are so good at catching butterflies! This is your third one this week! What would you like to name him?"

"I really want to name him Fred. He kind of looks like a Fred, don't you think Alia?" Kenzie looked up expectantly at Alia.

Alia looked at the butterfly and smiled. Its wings were purple, yellow, and a hint of white. If anything, Alia would have thought a girl's name would be best. But she looked down at Kenzie's dear little face, and said, "Yes sweet-heart, Fred would be a perfect name for this butterfly. Now, we need to release him back into the wild."

"Ok, I can do that." With her arms outstretched, Kenzie let him go. Then Alia had a thought. "Does God do that? Does He hold me for a while, and then just let me go?" Sometimes it felt like that. She definitely understood the "being in the wild" part of it. She sure hoped that God would still hold on to her. She knew the feeling of being "let go", and honestly, she did not like that feeling at all.

Her thoughts came to a halt when Kenzie's little brother Danny came running to her. "Le-le, can we go swimming today?" he asked hopefully.

"I think we can, Danny." Alia answered with a smile.

"Yippee! I am so excited!" After hearing that, he jumped up and down.

A thought went through Alia's mind. "Thank you God, for giving me this job of taking care of such precious kids." Then she realized that that was the first conversation she had had with God in some time. It may not have been much, but she really liked it. She wanted to tell Him more. Maybe after two excited kids jumped in to the pool.

"Would He really listen to me? I have failed living the 'Christian life.' Or have I? I don't know; I am a little confused." She thought to herself.

With the water splashing all around her, and two lively kids to look after, the afternoon was soon gone. Before she left with two tired kiddos, she was able to float on her back. With the bright sun upon her face, and the gentle, quiet water around her, she came to a conclusion. She would try talking to God, she really would. If He would want to listen to her, then she decided she would talk to Him. What she would say, she didn't know. But she would try. She really would.

When Alia got home, there was a message on her phone. It was from Jacie.

"Alia, guess what? There is an awesome band playing at the club tonight. Do you want to get all dressed up and go with me? Let me know if you want to go! Bye!"

Alia's heart just sunk. It would be fun to go out with Jacie. But she didn't really want to go. She was torn and conflicted, and didn't know what to do. She decided to go for a little walk before she talked to Jacie. She needed to think things through.

There was a little walking trail behind her apartment complex, and as she walked she just admired all the beautiful creation around her. The trees were lusciously green, the grass was soft and inviting, and the bright sun was shining down on her. She felt like she wanted to talk to God, so she did.

"God I want to know You, and I want to follow You. But I don't know how. I want to start making better choices, but it is hard for me to say no to Jacie." Then she realized something. She had a Bible in her room. Maybe that was a way to draw closer to God. She decided she would read it when she got back.

She decided to enjoy the walk back to her apartment, but something was making her feel kind of bad. She got to thinking about her past, and it upset her. For some reason, memories started

A Gift For Alia

flooding back. They were memories of past boyfriends, and hard times with them.

"What is going on? I just started talking to God, and now all these memories are coming back? I don't understand it God. I think I need some help. But where can I go?" All of a sudden, her Mother's sweet kind face came to her mind.

"Yes, that's it! I'll go to Mom and Dad, and talk to them. I know they can help me." With a smile on her face, she got to her apartment, and ran to her room. She opened the last drawer of her dresser and pulled out her pink Bible. It had been a long time since she had read it, but when she opened it, it fell to Psalm 4, and she started reading verse 1.

"Answer me when I call, O God of my righteousness! You have relieved me in my distress. Be gracious to me and hear my prayer."

"That's interesting," she thought to herself. "I love the part about asking God to hear my prayer. Will He really listen to me? I guess I will try talking to Him more. It should help me, and I don't think that it will hurt me at all."

14

Linda Sue Svoboda

Chapter 4

Maria and Henry were eating breakfast at their little table in the sunny, cozy kitchen. They ate together every morning before Henry went to work as a plumber. He had his Bible out, and also the comics. He read from each one daily, and it was good for him to start his day like that. Just then the phone rang, and Maria quickly got up to answer it. She was hoping it was her precious daughter. But it was someone else entirely.

"Hello? Yes, Margaret, I can hear you." Maria said with a sigh.

"Maria, I am most disappointed in your daughter. Why, she hasn't been in church for a month! And then we see her last Sunday, but she didn't want to say hi, or talk to anyone. The poor child's face was just ashen during the sermon, and it should be filled with joy! Joy because we all need to be in church, and Joy because that is what good Christians do!" Margaret said strongly.

"I am just glad that she came, Margaret. I'm happy that she wanted to come, with her busy schedule. Since you are concerned for her, please just pray for her. That would help the most." Maria said.

"Well, I surely will! I will put her at the top of my prayer list! I do pray for about 3 hours a day. I feel it is a Christian's duty to pray at least that much! How many hours do you pray in a day Maria?" Margaret asked smugly.

"Honestly Margaret, I don't keep track of how long I pray. I just pray throughout the day, whenever God puts someone upon my heart. I talk to Him while I walk outside, I share my feelings with Him while I am folding laundry, and I praise Him when I think of all my many blessings. It is just an ongoing conversation with Him. I know He is there all the time, and I love being with Him. I need to let you go now. Thanks for calling Margaret."

"Good-bye Maria," Margaret said.

Maria did not know if what she said would help Margaret understand giving others grace, or if it would help her to see that there are other ways to pray. But there was one thing that was on her mind.

"Henry, I think we might need to look into another church," Maria said hopefully. "I can't believe how mean people can be to our daughter. I know that she has had so many struggles in her life, and with her faith. But people should be encouraging at church, and not judging her. I was so happy that she made it to church, but I guess I see it in a different way. I see that she is taking baby steps towards God, but others see it as a way to put her down for not doing what is 'expected.' I pray for her so much, that she would see the truth, and know how much Jesus loves her. That is my heart's cry as her Mom, that she would see how much Jesus really loves her."

"You know, Maria, I have been thinking that for a while now. I'd love to find a church where grace flows freely." Henry said truthfully.

"Let's start looking this Sunday. I heard of a new church that started up a few months ago. It is just on the other side of town." Maria said thankfully.

"Yes, dear, I think that would be a good thing. I really do."

The doorbell rang just then, and Maria jumped up to answer it. As she opened the door, and saw her precious daughter there, her heart raced with love for her.

"Hello sweet-heart! It is so good to see you!" Maria gave Alia a big hug.

"Hi Mom and Dad, I really need to talk to you both. I have a bit of a problem, and could use your advice." Alia said honestly.

"Go ahead honey. I'll call work and tell them I will be a bit late," Henry said.

Alia began slowly, "I have been going to the bars and night clubs because I absolutely love to dance. I have had a lot of dates as well. Mostly they are men that you would not approve of, I'm sure. But I am tired of it. I'm tired of the smoke and the alcohol flowing freely. I'm tired of having dates that don't care at all

about me. I'm tired of going to those places on the week-ends."
Alia looked at her parents and saw faces filled with compassion.

She continued, "I thought I should go to church. So I did. But I didn't have anyone come up to me and say hi. I was waiting for just one person. Just one. But nobody came. I saw the whispers and glances at me. I saw the disapproving stares. It hurt. It really did. So I started talking to God on my own. I took a walk with Him. I just told Him how I felt. My question to you is, 'Will He hear me? I have messed up so much. Will He even want to talk to me?'" And with that Alia burst into tears. Her Mother put her arms around her and just held her while she cried. She cried and cried, and as she did, she felt the burden gradually lifting. She felt the love of her parents, and she so needed to be here. It was a place where she was loved and not judged.

"Oh honey, God is close to the broken-hearted and He does hear your prayers. Do you remember when you were a little girl, and you asked Jesus into your heart?" her Mom gently asked.

"Yes, I do. But that was so long ago." Alia sniffled a little bit.

"Alia, Jesus promised that He would never leave us or forsake us," her Dad said. "And always remember that Jesus is holding you in the palm of His hand. Then God the Father wraps His arms around Jesus holding you. You are secure in His love, and you can rest in His arms." Henry smiled a gentle smile.

"But what about everything I've done? I haven't exactly been a model Christian," Alia said sadly.

"Who is? Alia, the only perfect one is Jesus. Listen to me, honey, we all make mistakes. We all do wrong things. That's where forgiveness comes in. You can ask God to forgive you and He will! He promises to forgive, and that is such a beautiful thing! The fact that you want to grow closer to Him is wonderful. God sees your heart and sees that you are turning to Him. And I'm sure that makes Him smile." Her Dad said with conviction.

"You know Dad; I've never thought of God smiling at me. I like that thought. I really do. Thanks for listening and for helping me. I love you guys," Alia said with a soft smile. And with that, she gave them each a big hug.

18

Linda Sue Svoboda

Chapter 5

As Alia drove back to her apartment, she found that she was feeling quite peaceful. She was really glad that she went to her parents' house and talked to them. Just then, she remembered Jacie's phone call. She really needed to call her back. She didn't feel like telling her no, and she knew that Jacie could be pretty persistent. That was part of the reason that she had gotten messed up in the first place. She started talking to God about it.

"God, I really want to go to places that are pleasing to You. But I really like Jacie, and she is one of my best friends," Alia prayed. Just then, Alia thought about asking Jacie to the outdoor jazz concert that she had heard about. It was held at a beautiful garden, and everyone brought snacks and enjoyed the relaxing outdoors. Maybe Jacie would want to go to that. It was worth a try. She picked up the phone, and waited while it rang. Suddenly, Jacie answered.

"Hey Alia, do you want to party tonight with me?" Jacie asked excitedly.

"Well, actually, I was wondering if you wanted to go to an outdoor jazz concert with me? It is in the gardens downtown. I went to it a few years ago, and it was incredible. The musicians were amazing, and we can even bring a picnic supper! I'd really love to go to that instead," Alia said softly.

"Um, okay. I guess we could do that. Are you sure you don't want to go to the club?" Jacie tried again to convince her.

"Yes, I'm sure. I'll tell you more tonight, but I would really love to hear these jazz musicians. And it is a beautiful day. Spending time outdoors would be so relaxing." Alia answered confidently.

"Ok, you've made up my mind. I'll give it a try." Jacie said.

A few hours later, both girls were enjoying the gorgeous outdoors. As they listened to the soothing music, Jacie started talking to Alia.

"Alia, I've noticed something different about you. There's a peacefulness about you. I don't understand it, but I really wished I had some peacefulness in me." Jacie said wistfully.

"Well, Jacie, I can honestly say that one thing I'm doing differently is that I'm talking to God more." Alia said truthfully.

"Oh, I wouldn't have guessed that. Well, to each his own. That's definitely not for me. But if it works for you, great!" And with a smile, Jacie closed her eyes and swayed to the music. Alia felt a little sad, because she knew that her friend would find peace talking to God as well. She looked at Jacie and thought to herself," What a free spirit she is. But I'd rather have my spirit belong to someone. And I am very thankful for that Someone, as He is the One giving me the peace that I need. And boy, do I need it!" Alia said to herself as she listened to the relaxing music.

Chapter 6

Blake was in a hurry this morning, as he needed to get to work. Unfortunately, his car had a flat tire about 4 blocks from his work.

"What a bummer," he thought to himself. He called his boss and said he would be a bit late. His boss understood because Blake rarely missed work or was late.

As Blake stepped out of his car to look at his tire, he looked up at the sky. Even at 4:50 in the morning, he couldn't believe how beautiful the sky was. It was very dark, but you could see the stars shining.

"God, I am amazed at how perfect Your creation is. Help me to get this tire fixed." Thankfully, he had a spare tire. As he knelt down to get the process started, he noticed an old, beat up pick-up come up behind him. An older gentleman came out of the truck.

"Can I help you there, son?" the kind looking gentleman asked.

"Sure, that would be great! You look so familiar. I think I know you from somewhere. I remember now. I've seen you at the nursing home where my grand-mother is."

"Yes, that is true. My wife of 55 years is there. I go to visit her every day. Sometimes she recognizes me, and sometimes she doesn't. I just keep hoping that there are more good days than hard ones." he said with emotion.

As they got the tire on, Blake asked," How do you keep going? Knowing that there may be some days that are really hard?"

"She's my beautiful bride. She faithfully took care of me and our 5 kids without complaining. She was always there for me.

Now, I need to be there for her. We have had so many wonderful years. I just keep focusing on all the amazing times we have had, and I just go to be with her. That's what I feel I need to do," the gentleman said passionately.

"You know, that's my dream. I would love to find someone that I can spend the rest of my life with. It would be great to have someone that I can share the good and the bad with, and to have someone that I can talk to about everything. How wonderful to have someone to have a family with and to have someone who will be my best friend. How great it would be to have someone who I can grow older with. That's what I would love. How did you happen to meet her?"

With a nice smile, the man said," I tried to meet girls at all kinds of places. But I wasn't meeting the right kind of girls. I wasn't meeting the kind of girls that I would love to meet my parents. So I got some great advice from my Pastor. He told me to pray about it. So I did. At first, nothing happened. But I kept praying about it. And you know what? I met her. She was sitting in a park reading, and I was taking a walk after I had finished my classes for the day at the University. I thought she was the most beautiful girl I had ever seen. She looked like an angel, with her golden hair curled around her shoulders. I got up the nerve to say hi, and she was so friendly. I asked her out for a date, and the rest is history."

"That is really a wonderful story. By the way, I'm Blake. I'm sorry, I didn't even ask for your name," Blake said sheepishly.

"That's ok. It's Sam."

"I am going to try that, Sam. I'm going to start praying for my future wife. I don't know where she is or who she is, but I am going to start praying for her. Thanks for the advice, Sam. Also, thanks for helping me with this tire. That was really nice of you to stop, "Blake said thankfully.

"That's all-right. So many people have helped me throughout the years. I feel like helping others is what the Good Lord wants me to do these days. I hope you have a great day, and you are most welcome. "With that, Sam got into his worn out truck, and drove down the road.

A Gift For Alia

With a wave, Blake stared at the pick-up as it rambled down the road. "I'm starting to believe in divine appointments, God. That man was incredible, and I know that you made sure that he said just what I needed to hear. I am going to start praying for her. I don't know who she is, where she is, or what she looks like. But I'm going to start praying for her. I really am. And I am going to start now." With that, Blake got into his car, and prayed all the way to work. He knew she would be special. He just hoped he would be special to her as well.

24

Linda Sue Svoboda

Chapter 7

As Maria got ready to go to the new church on a beautiful Sunday morning, she almost felt like she was back in school again. She had nervous stomach jitters. She looked over at Henry, calmly reading the Sunday comics, and smiled. Not much riled up her sweet husband of 21 years.

"Henry, how did you get ready so quickly? I can't seem to figure out what to wear today. I feel a bit nervous." Maria said quietly.

"Oh, honey, you look beautiful in everything you own! Remember that we are going to worship God, and the whole point to going to this new church is to know more about Him," Henry said with a smile.

"You're right darling. I have been thinking about myself too much. It is all about Him, isn't it?" Maria said gently as she finished getting ready.

"It is honey. It really is. Let's go learn more about him." With that, Henry took her hand, and they headed out the door.

The church was on the other side of town, but they talked excitedly about what The Community Church would be like. As they pulled up to the new church, they noticed that there was a gentleman in the parking lot. He had a huge smile on his face as he directed the people where to park.

"That was nice," Maria commented to Henry.

As Maria and Henry entered into the door, a happy couple greeted them. "Welcome and good morning! We are so happy that you could join us. Please tell us a little about yourself."

"My name is Henry, and this is my wife Maria. We have one girl who is 21. Her name is Alia."

"You will have to bring her next time! We are so glad that you are here! Pastor Dave is incredible. His love for Jesus is beautiful, and his messages are practical and Bible based. Welcome to both of you!" the couple said happily.

A nice usher helped them find a seat in the middle of the beautiful church. Huge stained glass windows on the side of the church streamed light into the building. There was a wooden cross behind the altar. Immediately, Maria felt a peace as she took a deep breath. Worship time was incredible, as all the songs pointed to the cross. Then a very young looking guy got up and started to speak.

"Good morning everyone, I'm Pastor Dave. It is so good to see you all today. I'd like to talk about a topic that is near and dear to my heart. It will be a 2- part sermon. It is on the topic of forgiveness. I would like to share not only how God forgave me, but also how God helped me to forgive others. I've been through a lot, and made a lot of bad choices in my teen and college years. I was way down at the bottom of my life because I gave into temptations of drugs, alcohol, and girls. I just felt awful about myself, and my life. I spiraled down into a deep depression. I couldn't get out of bed in the morning because I was so sad, weak, and down and out. My sister ended up taking me to the hospital."

"At first, I didn't want to go, but I am so glad that I did! That hospital experience changed my life! I received treatment for my depression, but also I received spiritual help. You see, there was this pastor that visited the patients. He was a man with a quiet spirit, and a nice countenance. He came twice a week to see all of us. He brought his Bible, and sat down at the cafeteria. The minute he opened his Bible, almost everyone in that hospital gathered around him. He read a passage, and answered questions. I was amazed at his patience with all of us, and for his love for his God. I decided right then and there, that I wanted to know this God. He talked about how God can forgive even the deepest and darkest of sinners. Well, that was me. And I thought to myself,' If God can forgive me, after all I've done, then I want to tell others about this amazing gift as well,' And that is where the healing started. It was in a hospital, with me battling depression."

"Also, that wonderful man gave me a New Testament Bible with Psalms and Proverbs. It was the first Bible I had seen, and I read it. Right then and there, I really read it. Cover to cover. Something clicked in my soul, and I felt Jesus' presence with me at that hospital. Not only did I receive the medical help that my body needed, but I got the spiritual help that my soul craved for. And I realized that when Jesus died on the cross for me, that all my sins were forgiven. Oh, my, what a revelation! They were gone from the east to the west. I can't emphasize enough how freed up I felt! It was absolutely incredible! Since then, I need His forgiveness all the time. And He freely gives it to me! When I mess up, I know I just need to ask Him for His help and His grace. His forgiveness flows beautifully to me," Pastor Dave said honestly.

"And the best thing is that it can happen for you too! All you need to do is talk to Jesus and tell Him you believe in Him, and what He did for you on the cross. You can receive His forgiveness, and can begin a relationship with Him. He wants to talk to you and He wants you to talk to Him. "

Maria and Henry sat up in their chairs. "I've never heard anything quite like this honey," Maria said quietly.

"I know. This is an amazing message. I so wish Alia was here," Henry said. "We can invite her to come next week."

After the beautiful message, Maria and Henry walked towards the pastor. He welcomed them with a huge smile.

"Good morning! We are so glad that you both could come! I'm Pastor Dave." He said happily.

"Hello, I am Henry and this is my wife, Maria. We are so thankful to be here. Honestly, Pastor, we have never heard a sermon like that. It means the world to us to know that all our sins are forgiven. It's just a very wonderful thing to think about." Henry said reflectively.

Maria piped up," We have a daughter who has made some wrong choices. She has been hurt by a lot of people very badly. I don't know if she fully knows Jesus, or understands what He has done for her. Just hearing about God's forgiveness is wonderful for me. I only wish she could hear about it as well. "

"She's welcome to come anytime. I'd love to meet her, and visit with her. This is a place of grace. No questions asked. We just want people to feel God's love and experience His grace and forgiveness." Pastor Dave said truthfully.

"Thanks so much Pastor. Could you please pray for our daughter Alia? Pray that she will come to church soon, and pray that she will experience God's forgiveness and grace in her own life?" Henry said with tears in his eyes. He just knew that the more people praying for Alia the better, and he just had a hunch in his heart that this Pastor might be the one to lead his precious daughter to the One who truly heals.

Chapter 8

Alia got back to her apartment after the concert and just started crying. She didn't know exactly why she felt so heartbroken, but she really was. Memories of past boyfriends started coming in her head. She just felt awful about it. And then, after she had had a good cry, she saw her Bible on her stand.

"I really need You, God. I know You have to be out there. Could you please listen to me?" As Alia was wiping away her tears, she felt a peace come upon her. She kept talking. "I really need You now. Please just hold me Jesus. Just hold me." And with that heartfelt cry, she lay down, and went into a deep sleep. She knew that somehow, she would feel better. And she felt that Someone was watching over her.

When Alia woke up the next morning, she felt relaxed and refreshed. "What a great night sleep," she thought to herself. She stretched out, and thought about her day. Today was the day that she would watch those two sweet kids.

She wondered which toys and books she would choose to take with her that day, as she liked to bring something new for the kids to play with. She quickly got dressed, and drove over to their house. As she parked her car near their house, Danny ran out to meet her.

"Le-Le, guess what? I found a grasshopper last night! Mom let me keep him, and he's in a jar on my dresser. Do you want to see? Do you? Do you?" Danny asked in an excited voice.

"Of course I want to see him! Let me say hi to your Mom first." Alia said happily

When Alia opened the door, she saw Sally, the kids' Mom, smiling at her. "Good morning Alia. Thanks so much for coming! The kids and I are so glad you can come! Go ahead and find whatever you want for lunch. I think Danny has a lot planned for you this afternoon, with his new grasshopper and all. He told me that he wanted to find food for it today. That should be fun for you, as I know you don't mind bugs at all." Sally said smiling.

"We will have fun, and I'm glad that I can help take care of them too. It helps me to be positive and cheerful, because honestly, Sally, I am going through a lot right now. Being with the kids helps take my mind off of the serious stuff. It really is a joy to be here." Alia said truthfully.

"I'm so glad too. Ever since their Dad died, it's been hard seeing them so upset. But since you started coming, they seem happier and more peaceful. I know it is because the games you play, the songs you sing, and the toys and books that you bring over. They love being with you so much! Just call if you have any problems or questions." Sally said as she went out the door.

"We'll be fine! Hope you have a wonderful day!!" Alia said. Just after Alia closed the door, Kenzie came down the hall. "Hi Alia! Can we go to the library today? I just finished my book." Kenzie said happily.

"Sure, we can do that! It will just have to wait until we find Danny's grasshopper some lunch!" Alia giggled and gave Kenzie a big hug. Alia knew in her heart that she was in the right place. Spending time with these kiddos was truly a gift, and it was a present that she enjoyed opening day after day. She truly enjoyed every minute of it!

At the library, Alia was smiling the whole time. She loved to read, and seeing the huge selection of books made her so happy! Alia called out to Kenzie, "Kenzie, do you know what the library reminds me of?"

"No, Alia. What does it make you think of?" Kenzie asked with curiosity.

"It reminds me of a huge shopping mall, only instead of clothes, it is filled with books. And instead of paying huge amounts of money, you can get everything for free!" Alia said happily.

"I've never thought of the library that way, Alia. But I think that's a great way to think about it." Kenzie said.

All of a sudden, Alia heard Danny speaking to her. "Le-Le, look at all the books I've found!!" Alia turned around and saw Danny with his arms covered with books.

"Let me help you, Danny." Alia said. Together, they carried the massive load of books to a table.

"Wow, Danny, that is remarkable!" Alia said with amazement.

"What does that mean Le-Le?" Danny looked puzzled.

"It means you picked out a lot of books, and I am very proud of you. It's wonderful to love books, and I can't wait to read them with you." Alia reached down and gave him a big hug.

"Let's go home and read Le-Le," Danny said happily.

"Yes, let' go home and read." Alia stated enthusiastically. That is just what they did. After finding food for Danny's grasshopper, they spent the whole afternoon on the couch. They read funny books, happy books, and picture books. They bonded, over books, and they loved every minute of it.

32

Linda Sue Svoboda

Chapter 9

Blake found himself getting to work earlier and earlier most days. He prayed all the way to work, and found that it was a great way to start his day. He wasn't too tired, and he enjoyed talking to God at the start of his day. His co-worker Martin saw him came up to him.

"Hey Blake, isn't this a crummy morning and a lousy job?" Martin said unhappily.

"Martin, it's a beautiful morning, and I'm thankful to have a job. It's all about perspective." Blake said truthfully.

"How do you do it, Blake? How do you stay so positive? All I can do to think negatively. I can't seem to have one positive thought. My mind feels like mush sometimes." Martin said unhappily.

"Well, Martin, I will be honest with you. Knowing God and talking to Him makes all the difference. I have struggled with negative thoughts too. But I've learned not to dwell on a negative thought. It just makes it worse. When a negative thought comes in, I reject it, and then turn it into something positive. It helps so much to focus on positive things." Blake said truthfully.

"Well, I still don't know how you do it, Blake. It's all I can do to get out of bed in the morning. Sure, I usually stay up pretty late with my buddies, but I just can't for the life of me, think any positive thoughts. My buddies swear and drink, and they talk about all the horrible stuff that is happening to them and in their lives. I don't like it much, but they are my best friends." Martin said sadly.

"Maybe you need to get some new friends, Martin." Blake said with a smile on his face.

"But I can't do that, Blake. They are my best friends, and I just don't want to desert them", Martin said. "And anyway, what would I do without them? What kinds of things would keep me busy? I couldn't handle not going out to the bars! I love drinking too much to quit that!"

"Ok, Martin, it was just a suggestion. I hope your day goes well, I really do. And Martin, I have one more thing to ask you," Blake said. "Would you mind if I said a prayer for you?"

"Uh, I don't know, Blake. No one has ever asked me that. I don't know if I really need it, but maybe it would be ok. Well, thanks, Blake. What do prayers do anyways?" Martin asked with an unsure voice.

"Martin, I will tell you what prayer has done for me. It has brought me so close to God. He rescued me when I was going through a very hard time. You see, my Mom died when I was a teen-ager. It was the hardest thing I have ever had to go through. I cried out to God, in pain, and just talked to Him. I would pray about little things and the big things. I knew God was listening to me. In all my pain, in all my anguish, I knew He was there for me. Since then, every day I find something to talk to Him about. I know He cares about me. And I know He cares about you too, Martin." Blake said with a smile.

"Wow, Blake, I had no idea. So who raised you?" Martin asked.

"My Dad did a great job, but it was my Grandma Dolly who nurtured me and loved me like her own son. I am so thankful for her. She moved in with my Dad and I after my Mom died. I love her so much." With that, Blake wiped away a few tears. "Anyway, that's enough about me, but I just wanted you to know that God does care for you, and about all the big and little things." Blake regained his composure, and smiled at Martin. "We better get to work. I'm glad that we both came early so we could talk."

"I really am too. You gave me a lot to think about. Thanks Blake." Martin said.

"You are welcome. Anytime you want to talk, I'm available." Blake said with a smile.

And with that, Blake turned around and headed for his spot in the factory line. All day, he thought about how God had blessed him in talking with Martin. He knew that God loved Martin so much. It was kind of like a parable that his Pastor had talked about a few weeks ago. Jesus is the Great Shepherd, and he was tending 100 sheep. One sheep went missing. Jesus left the 99 sheep in order to find the 1 sheep that was lost. He cared about that little sheep so much, and he looked and looked until he found him. Blake knew that that one sheep was him. He knew that Jesus rescued him, and that He cared so much about him. Sometimes he felt like he didn't have much of a testimony, as he had begun a relationship with Jesus when he was in elementary school. He had stayed clear of alcohol, drugs, and had always respected girls. But as he was praying about it one day, God put this on his heart, "See what I have protected you from. You do have an amazing testimony. I have kept you from so much."

Blake knew then and there that He wanted to share Jesus with everyone he met. He wanted them to know that Jesus indeed cares about every detail, and He does protect us from making bad choices. But what Blake wanted people to know first and foremost was that when we do make a wrong decision, God is there ready to forgive us. He knew that even though he had avoided a lot of wrong choices, he still dealt with pride and bitterness. He knew that those feelings were just as bad as other sins. It's why he needed a Savior, and boy, did he love Him ever so much!!

Linda Sue Svoboda

Chapter 10

Maria and Henry felt completely overwhelmed, in a good way, after coming home from the new church. "I have never in my life felt loved in a church like I felt in that one!" Maria said with amazement.

"I know, Maria. I felt the same way. The people there were so down to earth, and very friendly. It really made me feel great!" Henry said. "I almost felt like I didn't deserve to be there. Like, I was so out of place. There were people who truly cared about us. And then, Maria, when the sermon started and Pastor Dave started sharing his testimony, I just about broke down. You know my past, Maria, and yet you looked past it. You loved me and forgave me for all the times that I have goofed up." Henry said with unshed tears in his eyes. "But you loved me, Maria. You loved me. Just like Pastor Dave said that God does. You loved me like He does. I was completely blown away by hearing that message." And with that, Henry started wiping tears away from his eyes.

Maria quickly went to his side. "Oh, Henry, of course I love you. I have loved you since we have been together 21 years ago. And yes, I forgive you. It's easy to forgive you because I know how much I've been forgiven myself. I have anidea, Henry. That idea is that we could share a little about what we've struggled with in our past with Alia. Not details, honey, but just how far God has brought us. I know she is struggling, and it breaks my heart. But if we shared with her what we have learned from our past, that may help her with her future." Maria said confidently.

"You are right, Maria. Let's have a picnic and invite Alia. It's such beautiful weather now, and we could play frisbee golf, eat, and talk. That would be great." Henry said to Maria, "Would

37

you like to call our precious girl, or should I?" With a smile, Henry turned to Maria's outstretched hand, and gave her the phone.

As only a mother could do, Maria asked her girl to go on a picnic with them.

"I'm really tired from my day with the kids, but I will be happy to go on a picnic with you and Dad. When do you want me to head to the park?"

"How about we meet at 6:00p.m.? Could you bring some chips or fruit?" her Mom asked.

"Sure, I can swing by the store on my way there", Alia said "I'll see you soon."

Alia got ready quickly by putting up her long brown hair into a ponytail, and headed to the grocery store. She absolutely loved being in this store. It had a huge selection of fruits and veggies, and she was thankful for that as she had been a vegetarian for several years. And there was one produce guy that she liked to talk to whenever she was getting her fruits and veggies. His name was Calvin and he was there that afternoon.

With a smile on his clean-cut face, he came over to Alia. "Hello. It's so nice to see you again."

"Hi! Do you happen to have any mangos? I'd like to make a fruit salad with strawberries, mangos, and bananas. And besides, I've been kind of craving them." Alia said shyly.

"Sure, we have a new shipment of them. They just came today. They must have been calling your name, because no one else has bought any yet." Calvin said to her with amusement.

"Thanks, uh, I don't think I know your name," Alia said

"It's Calvin. And you are?" he asked her.

"Alia. My name is Alia. It's short for Amelia. I'm named after my great- grandmother. "

"It's a beautiful name for a beautiful girl." Calvin stated.

"Thanks Calvin. Well, I'd better get going now. Thanks for all your help." With a smile, Alia turned around. She smiled to herself as she started walking away.

"Wait, Alia. Would you like to go out for coffee and scones sometime with me? "Calvin asked hopefully.

"Sure, that would be great." Alia said. Calvin smiled widely at her and asked for her number.

After she gave it to him, she turned around, she said good-bye. She wondered if this guy could be different from the rest. Maybe, but for some reason she was really looking forward to finding out. She really was.

Alia headed out to the park, and she realized that she was really excited to meet her parents for a little picnic. As she parked the car, she wondered where she would begin, as she had so many things she wanted to tell her parents. She headed up the green, grassy hill, and thought about the beautiful day. The sun was shining, the birds were singing, and the park was not too crowded. She felt a sense of peacefulness and calmness. She realized that she knew the Creator of this gorgeous place, and she felt close to Him.

"Help me to have a wonderful time with Mom and Dad, God. And then I pray that I can have time walking around and talking with You, Jesus. I really have a lot I need to talk about with You," Alia said.

She soon spotted her Mom and Dad, and ran to give them a big hug.

"Hi sweetheart," her Mom said happily.

"There's my girl," her Dad said with enthusiasm.

"Hi Mom and Dad! How are you both doing?" Alia asked happily.

"We are doing well honey. How are you?" her Mother kindly asked.

"I'm doing ok. I love my job with the precious kids, and I've been having pretty good energy. And I met a really nice guy at the supermarket a little bit ago. He wants to take me out for coffee and scones. But, Mom and Dad, the best part of my life is I've been talking to God more. Sometimes, I don't know what to say, so I just walk and enjoy what He's made," Alia said with a smile.

"Oh, honey, that is wonderful!! Talking to God is truly a beautiful thing. He cares about how you feel, and about what's going on in your life. He really cares about everything, and He loves you so very much." Her Mom said gently.

"Yeah, Mom, I'm finding out that I really like talking to Him." Alia said with a smile.

"Boy, I wish I had learned that at your age, Alia." Her Dad said. "I went through a lot of stuff on my own, thinking that nobody cared. But Someone did! He cared about me all the time. I just kept a lot of stuff inside when I was your age. I didn't tell anyone what I was going through. And it was rough, it was really hard. It wasn't until I met your Mom, and she started asking me questions. I hadn't even thought about these questions your Mom asked me."

"What questions did she ask, Dad?" Alia asked curiously.

With a wink at his beautiful wife, Henry said, "She asked me questions like,' When would I let my daughter date?' She asked me if I would feel comfortable talking with our kids about how we met? But the one question that totally threw me was when she asked me if I would let my 13-year-old daughter wear really short shorts if that was the style."

"Oh, Mom," Alia started laughing.

"I just wanted to see how he felt about things that were important to me," Maria said as she laughed too. "I guess they were kind of funny things to ask."

"Oh, honey, the questions were all-right. I just had never thought about them before. But you know what? It was such a good thing, because you got me thinking. You really did. It was a very good thing!" Henry said emotionally.

"I'm glad that you think so, honey. I really am," Maria said. "Alia, it got us started on topics that were good to talk about. Our relationship was based on excellent communication. Maybe that's too formal, Alia, but we never ran out of things to talk about. Daddy lived about 2 hours away from me, so we would talk on the phone during the week. On the week-end, we would get together. Daddy would stay with Aunt Sophie, and we would get together during the day. He would come over around 8a.m., and we would spend the whole day together. We would talk while we went grocery shopping, we would share our hearts while on picnics, and we would just walk around the park and open our hearts up with each other. We fell in love with each other's hearts. Sure, I

A Gift For Alia

thought that Daddy was the most handsome man that I had ever seen, but we waited to have our first kiss until about 6 months after we started going together." Maria said fondly.

"It was worth the wait!" Henry said smiling.

"Yes, it was honey," Maria said while grinning at Henry.

"I wish I would have known this all before, Mom and Dad. I made so many mistakes while I've been dating, "Alia said as she looked down at the ground.

"Honey, I want you to know something, "her Mom gently said. "We actually got pregnant with you before we got married. We kept this from you all these years, but now we realize that we have made a mistake in not being more upfront."

"We should have told you sooner. Our reasoning was that we knew that we were getting married anyway. But that was wrong thinking." her Dad said quietly.

"You are the most beautiful, wonderful daughter that we could have ever had. And we are so thankful for you! But for the past 21 years, we have wondered if we were ever forgiven. Alia, God did something extraordinary last Sunday. You know the new church in town?" Maria said with excitement.

"Sure, Mom, I drive past it often." Alia stated.

"Well, Dad and I went to it last week. The Pastor's name is Dave, and he gave the most amazing sermon on forgiveness. I have never heard anything like it in my life. He gave his own testimony, and it's incredible! He made a lot of bad mistakes too, but he shared how he came to learn that Jesus forgives everything! He just wants people to be free from bitterness, unforgiveness, and regret. He wants people to know that God loves, forgives, and heals." Maria said with tears in her eyes. "Honey, would you like to come with us next Sunday?"

"Oh, Mom, that sounds amazing. I just don't know, though. I guess I could try it out. I just don't want to get hurt again." Alia said truthfully.

"Honey, it's nothing like our old church. The people are welcoming, smiling, and really happy to see new people." her Dad said nicely.

"All right, Mom and Dad. You have convinced me. I will go with you. What time do I need to be ready?" Alia said.

"We'll come pick you up around 10 a.m." Dad said as he gave her a huge hug.

Her Mom said, "I love you honey. We have been praying for you, and know that God loves you so very much too."

Across town, Calvin was super happy. Alia was the girl of his dreams. She was smart, funny, and very beautiful. And best of all, she was available! He somehow couldn't believe his luck. Suddenly, he heard his Mom banging pots and pans in the kitchen.

"Ma, could you stop making so much noise?" Calvin yelled.

"Just cover your ears, boy. If you want your supper, stop begging me to be quiet!" his Ma yelled back.

"Oh, brother, "Calvin muttered under his breath, "Just what I don't need, a lot of noise right now."

"Ma, I have to get ready. I'm going out right now." Calvin yelled again. "I don't want your supper. I just need to get ready and go."

"Boy, I didn't raise him to be so disrespectful. It makes me kind of sad." His Mom said quietly.

"Well, Ma, I'm going now. I'll see you in a few hours." And with that, Calvin slammed the door and walked away. He actually couldn't wait to get away from his house, and he didn't think there was anything wrong with that.

He got into his car, that was practical, and yet not very clean. He didn't mind though, and didn't even care to think if Alia would mind.

Meanwhile, across town, Alia was getting ready. She was looking forward to getting to know Calvin better. But when Alia saw Calvin pull in with his dirty looking car, she felt a twinge of disappointment. Then she said to herself, "It's not what's on the outside that matters, right? It's what's on the inside that counts. She really hoped that the person that was in the inside of that dirty car would truly be a person that she wanted to know better. When Calvin stepped out of his car, he nearly ran to the door, because he was so excited. As Alia heard the bell, she took a deep breath, and opened the door.

"Good evening Alia," Calvin said nervously. "You look very nice."

"Hello Calvin," Alia said. "Thank you very much. Where are we going today?"

"I am going to take you to a fun burger joint, and then I have a surprise place that we are going to go to."

"Ok," said Alia. She had an uneasy feeling in her stomach. But she pushed it aside and hoped all would be well.

As Calvin reached Ed's Burgers and More, he began talking, and it was all about himself. "You know, Alia, I didn't graduate from high school. I just don't think an education is important. Making money is where it's at. My job at the grocery store brings in enough for me, but my Ma would like to see more of it. The way I see it, is that I made it, so it's my money. I get to spend it. It shouldn't go to house hold items; it should only go to what I want to spend it on. Why should I be told how to spend my money?" he asked while he took a gigantic bite of his burger.

Alia noticed that he didn't chew with his mouth closed, and her stomach lurched a little. She turned around and took a deep breath. All of a sudden, Calvin asked, "What do you do for fun?"

Alia couldn't believe it, "Did he really just ask a question about me?" "Well, I babysit two wonderful kids during the day. We do a lot of fun things, like swimming at the pool and going to the library. I love to go to outdoor concerts, but my favorite thing to do is go for a walk with God, "Alia said with a heartfelt smile.

At that, Calvin spit all the pop that he had been drinking out of his mouth, and he sprayed pop all over the place. He sat up, and said, "You do what?"

Alia was a little frazzled, but she said with confidence, "Well, I like to walk by the lake. And while I walk, I talk to God."

"You mean, like He's there?" Calvin was clearly confused.

"Yes, I believe that he's there. I believe that He's everywhere." Alia answered.

Calvin muttered something under his breath, and then got very mad. "I don't believe there is a God. How can you think that He is even out there?"

"He is out there, and He is very real to me. I know that He is there, I really do!" Alia almost had tears in her eyes. At that moment, she truly believed that He was there, listening. She knew in her heart that He was truly real, and a peacefulness and a calmness wrapped around her heart.

"Well, if you were my girl, I wouldn't let you talk to this God. How could there be a God when so many awful things happen in this world? How could he let my Pa just walk away from my Ma and me when I was so little? How could any God let that happen?" Calvin asked.

With that, Alia didn't know what to do or what to say. Then she felt that she should just say a little prayer for Calvin. So she did, and then she said this, "I'm sorry that happened to you, but you have to realize something. God is close to the brokenhearted, and God has compassion on what happened to you. He really cares about you, Calvin. I know if you'd try talking to Him, you would know that He is real. I'll pray for you, Calvin. But now, could you please take me home? I'm not feeling the best."

"Sure, I can do that. But don't you want to go to my surprise place? I was going to take you to the junkyard and we can look at old cars. Would you like that?" Calvin asked hopefully.

"No, I don't think so. Just please remember what we talked about Calvin." Alia said.

After Alia got home that evening, she thought of calling Jacie, but then thought that she would probably agree with Calvin's like of thinking. So she called someone she was rapidly thinking of as one of her best friends. She called her precious Mom. She laughed, she cried, and she was truly real with her. After Alia hung up with her, she realized what a treasure her Mom was. And she was thankful. She really was.

Chapter 11

Alia got home just as the phone was ringing. She ran to get it, and said," Hello?"

"Hi Alia, it's Jacie. Can we hang out sometime? I miss you so much. It's not the same to go dancing without you."

"I miss you too, Jacie. Sure, do you want to come over tomorrow?" Alia asked.

"I'd love to. I really have a lot to talk to you about."

Tomorrow came very quickly and after a good night sleep, Alia was so looking forward to seeing Jacie. When she opened the door, Alia went to give Jacie a big hug. "Jacie, it is so wonderful to see you! How are you doing?"

"I'm actually doing all-right. I haven't gone to the clubs that much. I've been doing a lot of thinking, and I have realized that I need to hang out in other places."

"Wow," said Alia. "How did you come to figure that out?"

"I've been watching you, and I have noticed that you seem happier, now that you have stopped going to the bars and dance clubs. I want what you have Alia. I seem to be just miserable, and I know that my life needs to change."

"I'll tell you, Jacie, I still love to dance, but I'm just dancing at my aerobics class at the gym. As for being happier, you're right, I really am. And I can honestly say that it's because I am spending more time with God. He has helped fill the void that I tried to fill with dating guys that weren't right for me, or dancing at the clubs. My Mom and Dad also invited me to a new church, and I'm going to check it out tomorrow. Would you like to come with me Jacie?"

"I'd love to come, but I don't know what to wear. What do people wear to church?" Jacie asked cautiously.

"Jacie, how about we were capris and a pretty shirt? Honestly, I don't know what people wear to this church, but I think that would be just fine." Alia said happily. She honestly couldn't believe it. Was Jacie just asking her about church? Did she really just ask that? Wow! Miracles really do happen, and Alia had a sense that even more wonderful things were going to happen. But until then, she would enjoy each and every day. Because that is what she felt she should do. Just totally enjoy life. It was so worth it.

Chapter 12

Sunday morning came very quickly as Alia noticed the sun streaming through her window. For some reason, she was actually looking forward to going to this new church. She felt like this would really be a new opportunity for her. She felt really excited about this. She got ready really quickly, and was amazed that Jacie wanted to come with her. She got an orange and oatmeal for breakfast, and headed out the door. She prayed that this morning would be good for both Jacie and herself. She went over to Jacie's house and found her friend feeling very nervous.

"It's okay, Jacie," She told her friend as she gave her a hug. "I think it's wonderful that you want to come with me. I will be with you the whole time." And with that they headed over to the brightly painted church. As they entered the beautiful foyer, they noticed a lot of smiling faces. A very friendly group of older ladies came up to them.

"Welcome girls! We are so glad that you are here! I haven't met you before. My name is Sandy. And this is Dorothy, Martha, and Mildred. We have an awesome program for young people, and you will absolutely love our Pastor Dave. He has an incredible story. Welcome to our church girls. We are so happy to meet you both." After that greeting, both Alia and Jacie started smiling too.

"Jacie, I think this is a place unlike any others. Do you feel a peace? Like this is a church that God blesses?"

"I do, Alia. I feel a warmth here. Let's go find a spot. Were your parents going to be here this morning?"

"Yes, they are planning to come. Oh, look Jacie, here they come!" Alia smiled widely and nearly ran into her mother's arms.

"Hi honey! So glad to see you too Jacie! Why don't we go and find a place to sit down? I'm so glad that you both have come.

It's quite an amazing place, "Maria said with a gentle smile on her face.

As Alia entered the sanctuary, she felt such a warmth come over her. She thought it may be the light streaming through the colorful stained glass windows, but then she realized it was coming from her heart.

"Could it really be all that different? Could I really feel Your love in a church, God? "Everywhere Alia looked, there were people smiling at her. And it wasn't just a curious, friendly smile. She could tell that it was a genuine, heart-felt, interested smile. And she realized that she was so happy to be there in that beautiful church. She couldn't wait for the service to start. She looked over at Jacie, and saw her friend shivering.

"Are you ok, Jacie?" Alia asked with concern.

"I think so, but I have never been in such a welcoming place before. I really don't know what to expect. I'm a little nervous, to tell you the truth," Jacie said.

"I am too Jacie. But let's keep an open mind. I have a feeling that this will be quite a service."

Alia looked at the front of the sanctuary and saw a beautiful wooden cross hanging from the ceiling. "Wow, God, I know that you are here. I can feel you." Alia prayed. When the choir started singing, Alia thought that she was hearing angels. She closed her eyes and just loved the melody. Soon, tears started flowing down her cheeks. The song was all about God's forgiveness, and Alia truly felt loved. She felt her Mom's gentle arms around her, and then Jacie was giving her a hug. She knew she was wanted and loved. All of a sudden, when the song was over, she felt another arm on her shoulder. She looked up and saw an older gentleman with the bluest eyes that she had ever seen smiling at her.

"Hello, my name is Walter. I've been praying for the new people that come to our church, and I just wanted you to know that God loves you. He has a wonderful plan for your life, and He truly cares about you," he smiled as he looked at Alia and Jacie. "You girls are precious treasures to Him. Know that you are very loved by Him." And with that, Walter smiled and walked away.

A Gift For Alia

"Alia, I've never heard anything like that. I've never been spoken to like that. It made me feel very special." And with that, Jacie started to sniffle.

"I know, Jacie. I can't wait to hear what the pastor has to say," Alia said expectantly.

A very young looking man in jeans and a sweater came up to the front of the church. He had a very nice smile, and he looked out over all the people gathered there.

"Welcome everyone, I am so glad that you could come here today. I want you to feel God's presence here, and I want you to know how much He loves you. He has shown me how much He loves me in the most surprising and unique ways. I can remember a time when I was recovering from a depressing day, and the doorbell rang. I went to get it, and there was a member from my old church with supper in his hand. This was somebody that I thought didn't like me. Boy, was I wrong! I was so surprised, and I didn't what to say; so I said, "Thank you so much! I wasn't expecting this. But it is so kind of you."

The older gentleman kindly said, "You are so welcome. I hope that you feel better soon." When he turned around, I asked him," Would you like to come in and talk for a bit?"

He said, "I would really like that."

We ended up having a wonderful chat. Turns out, he had family members that suffered with depression. Even with that, he still didn't know how to handle it when I had my bout of depression. I thought he didn't like me at all, but instead, he was dealing with his own issues. He told me he had been praying for me, and that he was sorry about what he had been telling people about me. He asked for my forgiveness. And of course I forgave him. That alone brought me so much peace. I can't tell you enough how that helped me! Forgiveness is powerful, friends, and if you want to have peace and joy in your life, then you need to forgive others. And sometimes you need to forgive yourself. That can be the hardest thing, but it is an absolutely wonderful experience. It totally frees you up! I'd like to share a beautiful verse with you.

"As far as the east is from the west, so far has He removed our transgressions from us." Psalm 103:12. That's what God does for us. He completely takes our sin away, and doesn't even remember it. And friends, that is what God wants us to do for others. He wants us to forgive those that have wronged us. Doing that will bring so much peace. And then leave it at the foot of the cross. If it does come up again, tell yourself that you have forgiven it, and change your thought. Pray that God will bring up good memories and focus on those good times. Also, if a bad memory comes up about your own past, forgive yourself and let it go into God's gracious hands. He will take it, and He will help you to just let it go."

Alia was holding onto every word, and just couldn't believe what she was hearing. "Could it be possible? Could she really be free from her past? Could God really forgive her? Was it really possible to forgive herself?" As the truth settled over her heart, she felt tears coming to her eyes. And then, they didn't just come up gradually, they started to overflow. She started sobbing, and soon felt her Mom's gentle arms around her. She prayed to God, and asked for His forgiveness for all she had done in her past relationships. She prayed and forgave herself for making mistakes. Immediately, she felt a peace surround her, and she felt God's presence around her. She looked up with tear-streaked cheeks, and saw the cross. She smiled. She totally understood what Jesus had done for her, and what price He had to pay for her to be forgiven. "Wow, God. Thank you so much," Alia thought happily. She smiled again, and it was a genuine smile. She looked over at Jacie. Her face was just ashen, and she was not smiling at all.

"Are you all-right Jacie?" Alia whispered with concern.

"I need to talk to the pastor. I've never heard anything like this, and I have a bunch of questions for him. My mind is a bit of a mess right now," Jacie said sadly. "I've been carrying all this baggage about my family and about my past. I didn't know that you can just ask God to forgive you. It's quite a thought, and it's one that I kind of like thinking about," Jacie was grinning just a bit now.

Pastor Dave went on to quote a few more Bible verses on forgiveness, and Alia thought she finally got it. Finally, she didn't have to carry the pain anymore. She knew she could just give it to

Jesus, and He would take care of it. How amazing that was! They sang another song, and then Pastor Dave thanked them for coming, and said how important it is to take the message to heart. He prayed and smiled, and said, "Have a wonderful and blessed day. God loves you so very much."

Across the church, there was a young man who noticed Alia. He saw not only how beautiful she was, but he also noticed her expressions during the service. There was something different about her, like she was something special. He knew in his heart that he wanted to get to know her, and he hoped that he could say hello to her today.

Alia looked over at her friend, and asked Jacie is she was all-right.

"I think I am, Alia. Can we go meet the Pastor? I would really like to talk to him." Jacie said nervously.

"Sure! I would love to meet him too. "Alia said.

Alia's Mom led them to the front of the church, and kindly said to Pastor Dave, "Thank you so much for your message. It really touched my life. I want to introduce to you my daughter, Alia. And this is her good friend Jacie."

"Hello Alia. Hi Jacie. I am so glad that you both could come. You are both welcome to come anytime. We have a Bible study class for young adults that meets on Tuesday nights. We would love to have you come! "Pastor Dave said.

Alia looked at Jacie, and saw her nodding her head. "We would love to come." Alia said thankfully.

All of a sudden, Alia turned around and saw a very nice looking young man glancing over at her. She especially noticed his eyes. He had the kindest eyes that she had ever seen. They were gentle eyes, and she had never seen any eyes like his. He smiled a slow, deep smile, and she knew it was just for her. Everything and everyone in the room stood still, and it seemed like it was just the two of them. Alia felt her heart beating fast as he came over to her.

"Hello, my name is Blake. I've never seen you here before. Is this your first visit here to the church?" Blake asked welcomingly. He thought that she was the most beautiful girl he had ever seen. With her long, brown hair curled around her shoulders, and her cheerful and easy smile, she was such a delight to see. He decided in his heart, that he definitely wanted to get to know her better.

"Hi Blake, my name is Alia. Yes, this is my first visit here." She said as she kept smiling.

"That's great! Welcome, and we are very glad you joined us today. I've been coming here since it opened a few months ago. Pastor Dave is amazing, and he is totally relatable. He is so real with his struggles, and with sharing his heart. I think that is why so many people come. There is a Bible study class for young adults that meets on Tuesday nights. Would you like to come?"

Alia turned around and saw Jacie smiling at Blake. It looked like she could have been drooling. "Of course, we will come!" Jacie said happily.

"Sounds great! See you then." With a nice smile, Blake walked away.

"Alia, did you see the way he looked at you?" Jacie whispered happily.

"I don't know. Maybe. He seemed nice, but looks can be deceiving. I may go to the Bible study, as it does seem interesting. But I am not here to meet guys. I just want to learn more about God." With a smile that wasn't too eager, Alia looked for her parents. She knew in her heart that Blake could be a nice friend, but she was tired of being hurt. Her guard automatically went up, and her desire to get to know him went the other direction.

Chapter 13

For some reason, Blake couldn't get that beautiful girl out of his head. He loved how she looked, and her sweet smile just swept him off of his feet. He had never felt this way about any other girl. There was something different about her, that put her apart from the other girls he had been friends with. He knew he wanted to get to know her better, but he decided to talk to God about it. He decided to go to the beautiful lake in town. It had a wonderful walking trail, where he could get some exercise too. He put on his comfortable tennis shoes, and headed out the door. When he got into his car, he turned on his radio, and a Christian Rap song came on. Other people may not like that kind of music, but for him, it was incredibly soothing. As he thought about the words, a tingling sensation came over him. He realized how much Jesus loved him, and he was so incredibly grateful. He soon arrived at the lake, and marveled at the crystal clear looking water. Huge trees surrounded the lake, and flowers were blossoming everywhere. The sun was shining brightly, and he took a minute to bask in the beauty of what all God had made.

Blake started to walk on the nice trail, and prayed in his heart. "God, I thank you so much for this time with You. Everything here is beautiful, and You made it all. I just have a burden in my heart for Alia. I would love to get to know her better, but I don't want to come on too strong either. Please give me the wisdom to know exactly how to pursue her." And then, he heard something in his heart.

"Just be her friend." Blake knew that was from God. He knew that because He had felt God speaking to him before. "Ok, God, I can do that. I will try to be her friend." With that, a peace suddenly came over him. He would take it slowly, and be her friend. He prayed that he could be the best friend she had ever had. And he knew Who to talk to about this, because God had been the best friend that he had ever had.

Chapter 14

Blake woke up feeling refreshed, even though it had been hard for him to get to sleep last night. He somehow knew that his life might change for the better, and he knew that he was going to enjoy every minute. He quickly got dressed, and drove his car to the nursing home. It was time to visit his Grandma Dolly, as he had a lot of questions for her. He was thinking through everything he wanted to talk to her about, and he just hoped he could remember it all. He really needed a female perspective on all the thoughts going on in his happy, yet muddled head.

As he pulled into the parking lot, he saw a couple sitting on the bench outside. The husband was sitting closely to his wife, and had his arm around her. She was looking at him as though he was the most handsome man on the planet.

"Such love," thought Blake. He walked up to them with a respectful smile on his face.

"Hello. My name is Blake, and I couldn't help but notice what a lovely couple you are. How long have you two been married?" Blake asked expectantly.

"My wife and I have been married for 62 years, and I have loved every minute of it. We have had hard times, but we have also had a lot of good times. For that, I am so very thankful," the man stated.

"If you don't mind me saying, there is such love in your eyes for each other. I would love to find someone who looks at me that way." Blake said wistfully.

"Young man, I will let you in on a little secret. Looks like that have to be earned. It comes from treating a woman with respect, and making sure that her needs come before yours. I met Evelyn when we were 17. I made a lot of mistakes because I had a lot of growing up to do. I went into the U.S. Army when I was 18, and even though I was on another continent, I could not forget her sweet face. I wrote her a letter every day, and she wrote me a letter every day. Did that ever make being separated a lot easier! She won me over with her kind and loving words, and her faithfulness to me. I knew I wanted to be faithful to her as well. When I was honorably discharged, I went to her father, and asked for her hand in marriage." He turned to his wife, and asked her, "Honey, do you remember when I asked you to marry me? "Evelyn looked up with tranquil eyes, and smiled at her husband. She then laid her curly white haired head on his strong shoulder.

Her husband continued, "I knew Evelyn liked small, peaceful gatherings, so I didn't want a lot of people over when I asked her to be my wife. I asked her out on a date, and brought red roses. She thought they were absolutely beautiful. I started counting them, and noticed that 1 was missing. I told her that I would step back outside and see if it had fallen outside. Seeing her smell my roses deeply really made me smile. After finding the rose, I stepped back inside the house. I gave her the last rose (it was artificial), and popped the top open. Inside was an engagement ring. It was simple, as I couldn't afford much, but her face broke into a huge smile. I had never seen her smile that big, and it warmed my heart. "Yes, yes, yes!!!!" She flew into my arms, and she has been in my arms ever since." And with that, he smiled, kissed his beautiful bride, and looked at Blake. With tears in his eyes, Blake smiled and told him, "Thanks so much, sir. I have never heard anything so beautiful. I really hope and pray that I will find someone so precious too." With that he went inside to talk to his sweet grandmother about advice on finding the right girl. He then realized that he just gotten some pretty incredible advice on finding the right girl, and he was so thankful.

He entered his dear grandmother's room, and saw his Dad on the chair beside her. "Hi Dad. Hi Grandma. So good to see both of you." His Dad got up, and gave his son a big hug.

"I'm so sorry I can't get up, my dear boy," Dolly said with a grin. "But my heart is leaping inside because you came to see me.

Blake had so much to tell his Dad and Dolly, but he didn't know how much to share. He was closer to his Grandma Dolly, but sharing with his Dad may bring them closer together as well.

After chatting about various topics, Blake got up the courage to ask his question.

"I had a question about a girl that I met. She is really nice, and I would like to get to know her better. But I don't want to scare her off either. I really want to be her friend first, before I ask her out on a date." Blake said.

Grandma Dolly smiled at her son, and said softly, "Sounds like how you were before you asked out Marilyn." Blake's Dad smiled and said wistfully, "Yes, it does." He looked over at his son and said, "Blake, I was scared stiff when I asked your Mom out on a date. The best advice I can give you would be to just be yourself. And ask her questions about herself. "

"Just don't be too pushy," Grandma Dolly said with a grin. "Girls like to have time to make up their mind if they want to go on a date with a guy or not. But the best advice I can give would be to just be her friend. Be the kindest, nicest friend that she has ever had. And if all you are to her is a wonderful friend, that is perfectly fine." Blake took a deep breath as he listened to his Grandma. This wasn't exactly what he wanted to hear. Then he quickly realized that he was hearing some wise wisdom, and he hoped he could be a wonderful friend to Alia. He really hoped that he could.

Linda Sue Svoboda

Chapter 15

Across town, there was a very excited girl trying on all sorts of outfits. She had no idea what people wore to Bible Studies. She tossed her shorter skirts, and low cut blouses on the floor. Towards the back of her closet was a beautiful sundress that her Aunt Tia had gotten her for her last birthday. She hadn't worn it yet, but with its neckline covered in ruffles, the floral print dress looked like it would be perfect. After she put her long, blonde hair up in a high ponytail, Jacie called up her best friend in the world.

"Hello?" Alia said.

"Hi Alia!" said Jacie excitedly. "Are you looking forward to the Bible Study?"

"I think I am," Alia said. "I just want to get to know God better."

"I just want to go and meet some nice guys! There are bound to be loads of them there." Jacie said honestly. She twirled around and looked around in the mirror. "What did you decide to wear Alia?"

"Well, I found a pretty dress in the back of my closet that I think will be appropriate. It is a long, black and white dress that I forgot that I had. I think it will be all right," Alia said with a little sigh. "I know that you really want to meet guys there Jacie. But I really want to grow closer to God. Maybe this Bible Study will help."

"Who knows, Alia. Maybe this Bible Study will not only help you learn about God, but it may bring you closer to a guy who loves God. I don't know, but please keep an open mind when it comes to being friends with guys at church. Especially to the handsome one who has his eye on you." With a smile, Jacie said, "Bye Alia. See you soon."

"Bye Jacie. I will pick you up soon." With a small smile, Alia truly wondered about what Jacie said. "Could there really be someone who loved God that wanted to be her friend?" The cry of her heart really hoped so. She really, really did.

Across town, Blake was getting ready for the Bible study as well. He was a little nervous and hopeful too. He hoped that Alia would be there, but didn't want to get his hopes up too much.

"I need to focus on you, Lord. But I would love to see her again. I know I need to just be her friend though. I really need your help God." With that little prayer, he finished getting ready, and got into his car.

Blake showed up at Pastor Dave's house right on time. He saw Alia and her friend from a distance. Alia looked beautiful with a nice dress that seemed to flow all around her. After that, he really didn't notice anything else.

Blake desperately wanted to hold the door open for Alia, but when Pastor Dave saw him, he asked him a question. "Hi Blake! Could you help me with the opening game? We are going to pick a paper out of a bucket, and answer the question on the slip of paper. I would like to pick you first. We have a few new people, and I think that it would be great if you could speak first. Would that be ok?"

Blake swallowed deeply, and said, "Sure, Pastor. That would be fine." Blake didn't know how much he could concentrate on the Bible study, but he prayed that he could be a good listener, and take some nuggets of truth home to his heart. For his heart had been feeling a little funny, and he could use some wisdom and guidance from God. He really could.

Pastor Dave welcomed everyone in, and said for everyone to find chairs. "Hello everybody. So glad that you are able to join us tonight." With a smile, he said, "We are going to pass around this bowl and you can each pick out a slip of paper. It begins with a question, and each paper will be our topic for different Bible studies throughout the year. Let's go around the room, and share what topics we are going to learn. Blake, can you share first?" Pastor Dave said.

Blake said, "What are some things you are thankful for?" Blake thought to himself that it was a good topic. He really did have so many things that he was thankful for.

60

Soon, all sorts of topics were being shared. "How does a person grow closer to God?" "How does someone know they are forgiven?" "What does the Bible mean to me?" "How can the past stay in the past?" "How can we be free from bitterness?" "How can memorizing Bible verses help my thought life?" Then, Alia, read her topic. "How can we know who is the right person to date?" Alia read her paper with a sigh. "Why did that have to be her paper?"

Pastor Dave smiled and thanked everyone for reading the topics. "These will be our topics over the next year. If it takes us 3 or 4 nights to finish a topic, that would be totally fine. We are going to be diving into the Bible, but we are going to go slowly. I want everyone to get these nuggets of truth that we will be digging out. Tonight, I'd like to talk about how to make the past stay in the past. We all have made mistakes, and want to be free from those burdens. Sometimes, a memory may come up, and it may make you feel quite awful. But when we know Jesus, He can take those memories, and heal them. Isaiah 1:18 says, "Come now, and let us reason together," Says the Lord. "Though your sins are as scarlet, they will be as white as snow; Though they are red like crimson, they will be like wool. "God can completely heal our past, and make everything new again. Also, what I like to do when a memory comes up is think about a Bible verse instead of dwelling on the memory."

Alia stood up in her seat. She had been struggling with this. She was wondering if she was going to have to struggle with bad memories forever. They were so incredibly painful. Would this way really work?

Pastor Dave continued, "Our minds are very powerful, and we need to dwell on God's grace and forgiveness. And His truth as well. My favorite verse to think about when a bad memory comes into my head is Philippians 4:8. "Finally brethren, whatever is true, whatever is honorable, whatever is right, whatever is pure, whatever is lovely, whatever is of good repute, if there is any excellence and if anything worthy of praise, let your mind dwell on these things." When we ask God to forgive us after we have made a mistake, He will forgive us. We can cling to the fact that we are completely and totally forgiven. We can rest in the fact that our sins are gone, and we are made new. He surrounds us with His wonderful love. That is how powerful our God is."

Alia was absolutely blown away by what Pastor Dave said. Then, she noticed someone sniffling, and noticed that it was her good friend Jacie. Alia pulled out a small pack of tissues from her purse, and handed it to her. Alia put her arm around Jacie's shoulder and gave her a gentle hug. She smiled a soft smile, and whispered to Jacie, "Are you doing ok?"

It was all Jacie could do to slowly nod. She whispered back to Alia, "I don't know quite what to think of this. Can this all be true? I really need to talk to Pastor Dave."

Alia looked at her best friend, and smiled. She knew that she needed to talk to Pastor Dave too. Maybe the two of them could both get some help in dealing with their pasts. She sighed, and knew in her heart that she really needed help, and now she knew where to get it. And she was so very, very thankful.

Across the room, Blake couldn't believe what he just saw. That beautiful girl helped her friend. Blake saw Alia shower her friend with compassion and kindness. He was able to see that Alia had a heart of gold. And he was hoping that he could win that heart, and get to know that lovely girl as well.

Chapter 16

After an hour of talking, reading, and finally understanding part of the Bible, Jacie quietly came up to Pastor Dave. With a timid smile on her face, she asked, "Pastor Dave, that was so amazing to hear. I would love to find out more about God's forgiveness, and His ability to wipe away all our sins and mistakes. I find it hard to believe that He could do that. Especially for me." Jacie wiped away a small tear.

"I am so glad that you came, Jacie. Yes, it is true. God does forgive us, when we ask Him. Would you like to meet this week, and we can talk about how God truly forgives us?"

"Yes, Pastor Dave, I would like that. I have never heard any of this before. This is actually the first church that I have been to. Except when my Great-Aunt Lola passed away. But that church wasn't too much fun to be at. I actually couldn't wait to get out of that one. This church is different. It's not stuffy, or filled with people who have cold, stern faces. The people here seem to be so nice. I really want to be here, and learn about God." Jacie said with a smile.

While Pastor Dave and Jacie were talking, Alia was a little confused. She knew that God loved her, and that talking to Him was great, but could these people really be different that those at her old church? Just then, a few girls came over to her. With cheerful faces, they said they were happy that she was there. They visited a few minutes, and then Alia noticed that the very handsome young man was starting to come over to her.

Alia was a little shy, but soon smiled as Blake smiled right back at her. "HI. I'm Blake. I am so glad that you came tonight. Your name is Alia, right?"

"Yes, it is. I'm really glad that I came too. Sounds like it will be a wonderful Bible Study." As Alia was talking, she again noticed something that was so unique in Blake. Compared to the other guys she knew Blake had the kindest eyes that she had ever seen. They were soft, and yet compassionate, and very kind. She kind of liked that. Other guys had such mean eyes, but Blake's eyes were so incredibly different. She felt like she could enjoy getting to know him, and she liked him a little already.

Blake was smiling down at her, and said, "I hope that you and your friend have a wonderful night. Will you be coming to Bible Study again?"

Alia nodded her head, and happily said, "I would love to come again."

"That's great! I will look forward to seeing you again then." And with a smile directed just for her, he turned around and walked down the steps. Alia watched him walk away, and thought that he may indeed be a very special guy. He was different. He had a quiet spirit in him. Then, she realized something. Could it be the fact that he knew God? Could that make so much of a huge difference? She didn't know, but she sure hoped that she could find out.

Chapter 17

As Alia drove to the house where she babysat the two precious kids, she heard something very interesting on the radio. A huge jazz band was going to be performing in town soon. They were her favorite band, and she would love to see them. She made a mental note to call the ticket office when she could.

Kenzie and Danny were full of laughter and playfulness that day. They asked nicely, "Le-le, could we please make cookies? We could make them for Mama. She is such a nice Mama."

"Of course, kids, we can do that. Let's get all the ingredients set out on the counter." Alia said.

Over the next hour, the kids got all the ingredients together, and they sang while they put the cookies on the cookie sheet. Alia told them stories of when she baked cookies with her Mom, and her Grandmother. She shared with Kenzie and Danny that her Mom and Grandma told her stories while they baked. She looked at those two sweet kids, and asked them, "Would you like to hear a story about me? One when I was your age?"

"We would love to!" They both said happily.

"Ok, I am going to tell you about my favorite place to sit as a little girl. "Alia paused as they looked very puzzled. "When I was younger, I loved to climb a huge oak tree in my front yard. In the branches, there was a perfect place to sit, and I felt so protected as I sat amidst the beautiful green leaves. You may have a perfect place to sit as well." Alia said gently.

"I have one Le-le!" Danny said enthusiastically. "It's in the back yard! It's by Mommy's flowers. They make me very happy."

Alia smiled. "Yes, Danny. That's a perfect spot for you."

Kenzie said, "I think my favorite spot is on our sofa, where I like to read my favorite books from the library."

Alia said, "It is wonderful to read Kenzie. The sofa is a great spot for you. While these cookies are in the oven, why don't you both spend some time in your favorite spots? We will relax and read this afternoon. I think that would be lovely."

The kids both smiled, and went to their special spots. Alia got her phone out, and ordered 2 tickets for the jazz concert. Even though she didn't go to the bars anymore, she thought she would always have a soft spot in her heart for jazz music. It probably came from the big band music that her parents listened to when she was growing up. She would spin around the living room, and imagine dancing with her husband to this beautiful music. Her hair would be up in a gorgeous style, and she would have a long, elegant dress on. Together, they would dance and sway, and all that would matter would be looking into each other's eyes. They would smile at each other, and know that the other one was the only one for a lifetime. This was one of her most treasured childhood imaginings. But she knew in her heart that it would happen for her. She didn't know when, but she just had a feeling it may be sooner than she thought.

Chapter 18

Blake was thinking a lot as he got ready for an amazing concert. He was so happy to hear this group of musicians. He had waited a long time to see them. He had wanted to invite Alia to come with him, but he didn't know if she liked this kind of music. He got to the Arena a little early, and found his seat. He saw that they were going to play a lot of his favorite numbers. Across the Arena, he couldn't believe what he saw. Alia was climbing up the stairs. She looked like she was by herself. Boy, did she look beautiful. She found her seat, and started reading the program. He could tell that she was smiling. Soon, the jazz band started playing. They were absolutely incredible! When intermission came, Blake went over to the side of the Arena where Alia had been sitting. He looked in the halls, but couldn't see Alia. "If only I got a chance to say hello, I will be thankful, God." All of a sudden, he turned around, and saw her. She turned as well, and saw him. "Wow, Lord, look at those kind eyes." Alia thought.

"Hi Alia." Blake said happily. "I didn't know that you liked jazz music."

"I love it. It's one of my favorite kinds of music. I have listened to it my whole life." Alia said truthfully with a smile.

"That is wonderful. I enjoy listening to it too." Blake said. "I have an extra seat by me, if you would like to join me. That is, if you weren't waiting for someone."

"My Mother was going to come, but she wasn't feeling very well. So, I came by myself. I have absolutely been loving this concert, though. Actually, I would like to take you up on your offer. That would be nice to sit by you." She looked at Blake with a happy smile. "He really is a great guy," she thought to herself.

Blake couldn't believe it, and yet, he could. He knew that God was an amazing God, and he knew that God had a plan for everyone. If all he was to her was a wonderful friend, he would be that friend. But the way that she smiled at him, and the way that he was smiling down at her, gave him hope. Hope that God did indeed answer prayers, hope that God cared about every detail in his life, and hope that dreams really did come true.

Epilogue

Alia's smile made all the difference to him. It was a tender smile, yet inviting. She looked absolutely beautiful, and she was smiling at him. He couldn't believe what he was seeing. She said yes! She actually did! How did he get to be so fortunate, and so incredibly blessed? Blake looked around this amazing church, and saw so many family and friends. They were already smiling, and wiping their eyes. And then he spotted his Grandma. She was sitting in the front row, wearing her best purple dress and hat. Tears were glistening on her cheeks, as she smiled widely at him. However, he could sense another person with a beautiful smile looking at him, and that was Alia. His precious girl, Alia, whom he loved with all his heart. God answered his heart's cry, and his deepest desire of finding a wonderful wife. He had spent hours with God, praying for a wife who loved Jesus with all her heart. He also prayed for someone that he could love from the bottom of his heart, and he found that with Alia.

Looking at her with her head full of curls, and her gorgeous white wedding gown, he was awestruck with wonder. How could he be so incredibly blessed? He just couldn't comprehend it, but he was so very thankful. He looked into Alia's beautiful eyes, as Pastor Dave started talking.

"Thank you all so much for coming today, and celebrating how God brought Blake and Alia together. It is amazing what happens when God answers prayers, and today they would like to share with you the miracle of their love for each other. Let's all look up to the screen, as we watch a little slideshow."

The whole congregation watched expectantly as the screen came down. Pictures of Alia as a little girl came up. There were the times when her Daddy held her as a baby, the time that she rode her first pony, her 3rd birthday party, her adorable smile when she lost her 1st tooth, her 6th grade graduation, sitting on the beach with her high school friends, and going on a cruise with her parents, as a present for her high school graduation. Blake's growing up years were next. There were pictures of his chubby, little face, as he smiled so wide. Other happy moments were shared. Pictures of going to the zoo with his father, and learning to cook with his Grandma. There was also a picture of his Mom, taken before she was sick. Her beautiful, wide smile was purely golden, and she held her precious Blake with strong arms. Blake started tearing up as he saw that one. "If only she could have been here, Lord." He whispered that prayer. "But I know that she is loving being in heaven with you. Please tell her that I am marrying the love of my life today."

Then, pictures of Blake and Alia started to flood the screen. Pictures of them dancing and smiling together were shown. There was that picture of them having a sweet picnic in the park, and them swimming together at the gorgeous, massive lake nearby. There was a picture of a huge sandcastle that they created. Then came the picture of them eating at a delicious Chinese Restaurant, and this one was so special. Here is where Blake got down on one knee and proposed to this beautiful girl. Blake looked at Alia, and held her hand. She smiled her soft and sweet smile at him. Blake still couldn't believe that this treasure of a girl would soon be his. His to love, his to cherish, his to protect for the rest of his life. It was a tall order, to be sure, but he was definitely up for the challenge. He would treasure this girl, his girl, for as long as he had breath. And he was going to love every minute of it.

As Alia looked at her precious Blake, the man who would soon be her husband, she felt her heart twirl a bit. She couldn't believe that anyone would want to marry her, especially after what she had been through. But that didn't matter to Blake. He knew that Jesus forgave her, and he had forgiven her too. When they had a huge conversation about it, he shared a verse with Alia, from Isaiah 1:18, (NIV) that had been near and dear on his heart.

"Come now, let us settle the matter," says the Lord. "Though your sins are like scarlet, they shall be as white as snow, though they are red as crimson, they shall be like wool." When Blake shared this with Alia, it felt to her like her whole world was new and alive. Suddenly, when she looked up, the trees looked a lot greener, the sky looked like it was sparkling, and the birds sang so cheerfully. Her whole world had changed. She found someone who truly didn't mind her past, just like her Heavenly Father, and she was so incredibly grateful.

As both Blake and Alia were holding hands and gazing into each other's eyes, Pastor Dave had a beautiful message for them. He talked about love, kindness, faithfulness, and forgiveness. He shared that it can only happen with God's help and guidance. They said their vows to each other. Alia promised to love, honor and respect Blake. She also said that she would provide a peaceful home, so that Blake would have a haven to come home to. Blake promised to love, cherish, and protect her. He said that it would be his joy to provide for her. But they both knew that whatever they earned, would be theirs' to enjoy together.

Then Jacie went up to sing a song. She was so pretty in her soft pink dress, and her hair was long and very straight. She was a little nervous, as she wanted to sing perfectly for her best friend's wedding. And she did. Her voice was strong and clear, and the songs that she sang were absolutely beautiful.

"How could this be? I can't believe Alia is getting married. We were always 'two peas in a pod.' "She thought to herself. Then she looked over at Blake and Alia. They were so adorable, and she wasn't too jealous anymore. "I am so happy for them," she said to herself with a little smile. "I feel a little sad too, because I don't like to be by myself. Will I be able to handle this? Should I be happy for them or sad for me? I kind of feel like I am losing my best friend. Maybe I am, but maybe I am not."

As Jacie pondered all of these things, Pastor Dave finished his message to the two lovebirds, and pronounced them husband and wife. "Blake, you may now kiss your bride." With a tender touch to his lovely bride's cheek, he kissed her very gently. Almost like she was a porcelain doll, and very delicate. After he kissed Alia, she looked up at him with a soft and happy smile. She was his, and his alone. She felt safe, she felt chosen, and she felt loved. It was a passionate feeling that she felt completely, and that she felt fully.

As they made their way up the aisle, Blake and Alia saw people that meant the world to them. They saw precious family members, treasured friends, and people that had been very kind to them. Truly, this will be a day that they will treasure forever in their hearts, and a day that they will always be very thankful for.

A Gift For Alia

74

Linda Sue Svoboda

www.ingramcontent.com/pod-product-compliance
Lightning Source LLC
Chambersburg PA
CBHW052120110526
44592CB00013B/1681